TASMANIAN DEVIL

AUSTRALIAN ANIMAL DISCOVERY LIBRARY

Lynn M. Stone

Rourke Corporation, Inc.
Vero Beach, Florida 32964

PHOTO CREDITS

All photos © Lynn M. Stone except title page © Australian
Information Service

ACKNOWLEDGEMENTS

The author thanks the following for photographic assistance:
Lone Pine Koala Sanctuary, Brisbane, Queensland, Australia

LIBRARY OF CONGRESS
Library of Congress Cataloging-in-Publication Data
Stone, Lynn M.
  Tasmanian devils / by Lynn M. Stone.

    p. cm. — (Australian animal discovery library)
    Summary: An introduction to the Australian marsupial whose
curious look has earned it an undeserved name.
    ISBN 0-86593-056-2
    1. Tasmanian devil—Juvenile literature. [1. Tasmanian devil.]
I. Title. II. Series: Stone, Lynn M. Australian animal discovery
library.
QL737.M33S76   1990
599.2—dc20   90-30483
                                      CIP
                                      AC

TABLE OF CONTENTS

THE TASMANIAN DEVIL

Is the Tasmanian devil *(Sarcophilus harrisii)* really a "devil"? The Tasmanian devil is really a mammal, a furry, four-legged animal. And it is a special kind of mammal, a **marsupial.**

Marsupials give birth to babies which are extremely tiny. Because they are so small, marsupial babies are raised in their mother's warm pocket of skin. That pocket is called a **pouch,** and it sets marsupials apart from other mammals.

The Tasmanian devil has sharp teeth and powerful jaws, but a devil it's not.

THE TASMANIAN DEVIL'S COUSINS

The Tasmanian devil is one of 258 marsupials. Its closest relatives are marsupial mice and squirrel-like marsupials known as quolls and "cats" in Australia.

Many of the marsupials live in Australia and the nearby island nation of New Guinea. The Tasmanian devil's only marsupial relative in North America is the opossum. Like other marsupials, the opossum mother has a pouch for her babies.

Virginia Opossum

HOW THEY LOOK

This animal with the curious name also has a curious look. No one would accuse the Tasmanian devil of being handsome.

The Tasmanian devil might remind you of a plump terrier or an overgrown rat. It has brown or black fur with a white throat patch. Its nose is pinkish white.

The Tasmanian devil's head is short and wide. Its tail is from nine to 12 inches long. Its body is from 20 to 31 inches long.

Tasmanian devils weigh from nine to 26 pounds.

Tasmanian Devil

WHERE THEY LIVE

Tasmanian devils live only in the Australian state of Tasmania.

Tasmania is a large island which lies off the southern coast of eastern Australia.

The "devils" live throughout Tasmania. Their home, or **habitat,** is usually a brushy or wooded area.

Tasmanian devils used to live on the Australian mainland, too. They began to disappear when dogs were first brought to Australia. Dogs had little trouble catching the slow-moving "devils."

Tasmanian Devil

Kangaroos, Australia's best known Marsupials

HOW THEY LIVE

Tasmanian devils are mostly active at night, like bats and most owls. This habit makes them **nocturnal.**

During its nocturnal, or nighttime search for food, the Tasmanian devil constantly sniffs the ground.

During the day, the "devils" hide in a shelter. It may be a cave, hollow log, brush, or another animal's den.

Tasmanian devils usually remain on the ground, but they can climb trees.

Tasmanian Devil sniffing ground

THE TASMANIAN DEVIL'S BABIES

A Tasmanian devil's mother has a **litter** of two to four babies. Each weighs just a fraction of one ounce when it is born.

The babies live in their mother's pouch for 15 weeks. There they grow by nursing on her milk.

By the age of two years, a female Tasmanian devil is ready for her own family.

The oldest known Tasmanian devil lived just over eight years.

Tasmanian Devil cleaning foot

PREDATOR AND PREY

Animals like the Tasmanian devil, with sharp teeth and strong jaws, eat meat. The Tasmanian devil also crushes and eats bones.

The Tasmanian devil is not a very skillful hunter, or **predator.** Its **prey,** the animal it hunts, might be a wallaby, wombat, sheep, or rabbit. But many of the animals that a Tasmanian devil eats are already dead when the "devil" finds them. This kind of food is called **carrion.**

In North America, vultures and coyotes often feed on carrion.

*Tasmanian Devil feeding
on small bird*

THE TASMANIAN DEVIL AND PEOPLE

Because of its name, growling, and sharp teeth, the Tasmanian devil is thought of as fierce. Eric Guiler, an Australian scientist, handled 7,000 Tasmanian devils. Mr. Guiler says the "devil" isn't as fierce as people like to think.

The Europeans who settled Tasmania killed thousands of "devils." They thought these animals killed their sheep and calves. In fact, the Tasmanian devil feeds almost only on sheep and cattle it finds dead.

Tasmanian Devil

THE TASMANIAN DEVIL'S FUTURE

By the early 20th century, Tasmanian devils had become rare. They were being shot, and their habitat was being gobbled up by settlers.

Tasmanian devils are still not widely liked. But they do have some protection now. They also have more carrion upon which to feed. That is the result of more farms in Tasmania.

The "devil" has begun to return in larger numbers in some parts of Tasmania. That's good news for the "devil"—and for everyone who enjoys this curious animal.

Glossary

carrion (KARE ee un)—old meat of dead animals

habitat (HAB a tat)—the kind of place an animal lives in, such as brush

litter (LIH ter)—a group of babies born together from the same mother

marsupial (mar SOOP ee ul)—a family of mammals in which females have a pouch for raising the young, which are born not fully formed

nocturnal (nohk TUR nal)—active at night

pouch (POWCH)—the mother marsupial's warm pocket of skin in which her babies are raised

predator (PRED a tor)—an animal that kills other animals for food

prey (PREY)—an animal that is hunted by another for food

INDEX